A Good Life
Benedict's Guide to Everyday Joy

Also by Robert Benson

Between the Dreaming and the Coming True

Living Prayer

Venite:
A Book of Daily Prayer

The Game:
One Man, Nine Innings
& A Love affair With Baseball

That We May Perfectly Love Thee:
Preparing Our Hearts for the Eucharist

The Body Broken:
Answering God's Call to Love One Another

A Good Life
Benedict's Guide to Everyday Joy

Robert Benson

PARACLETE PRESS

Brewster, Massachusetts

A Good Life: Benedict's Guide to Everyday Joy

2009 Fourth Printing
2007 Third Printing
2005 Second Printing
2004 First Printing

© 2004 by Robert Benson

ISBN: 978-1-55725-356-9

Library of Congress Cataloging–in–Publication Data

Benson, R. (Robert), 1952-
   A good life : Benedict's guide to everyday joy
      p. cm.
   ISBN 1–55725–356–0 (pbk.)
    1. Benedict, Saint, Abbot of Monte Cassino. 2. Christian life—
Meditations. I. Title.
   BX4700.B3B46 2004
   248.4'82—dc22

                        2003026115

10 9 8 7 6 5 4

Published by Paraclete Press
Brewster, Massachusetts
www.paracletepress.com

Printed in the United States of America

This book is for
my friends from Cedar Springs.

And it is for
The Friends of Silence & of the Poor,
wherever you may be

Contents

Longing

Seeking his workers in a multitude of people, the Lord calls out and lifts his voice again: Is there anyone here who yearns for life and desires to see good days?

Let us open our eyes to the light that comes from God, and our ears to the voice from heaven that every day calls out this charge: If you hear his voice today, do not harden your hearts.

We must, then, prepare our hearts and bodies for the battle of holy obedience to his instructions. What is not possible to us by nature, let us ask the Lord to supply by the help of his grace.

We intend to establish a school for the Lord's service. In drawing up its regulations, we hope to set down nothing harsh, nothing burdensome. The good of all concerned, however, may prompt us to a little strictness in order to amend faults and to safeguard love.

Do not be daunted immediately by fear and run away from the road. It is bound to be narrow at the outset. But as we progress in this way of life and in faith, we shall run on the path of God's commandments, our hearts overflowing with the inexpressible delight of love.

1

> *Listen carefully to these instructions, and attend to them with the ear of your heart. It is advice from one who loves you; welcome it, and faithfully put it into practice.*
> — From the Rule of Saint Benedict

Over the past eight or ten years, a number of people have been kind enough and curious enough and gracious enough to allow me to be a leader at retreats for some portion of their community or for some group that they gather together.

There is always this rather odd conversation somewhere in the months before the retreat, a conversation that is held between me and the person who is issuing the invitation.

"What will you teach?" they say.

"I am not a teacher, really," I say, hoping they are not too disappointed. "I am a pilgrim, and sort of a head cheerleader at such things."

"Well, then, what are you going to talk about?" they ask.

"We are going to talk some about the Rule of Saint Benedict, an ancient monastic rule, as a way of beginning to see our own lives more clearly. And we are going to look at the ways that we balance our prayer and our work and our rest and our relationships."

"What should I tell people that we are going to do?" they will say.

"Tell them that we are going to pray the daily office together, and we are going to be silent a good deal. We are going to ask and answer some hard questions, questions that involve really listening to our lives, questions about where our time and energy really go, questions about the things we long for and the things we love. In the end we are going to make a Rule for living our lives based on the wisdom of Saint Benedict's Rule."

"Oh," they say.

I can almost hear them wondering on the other end of the line: *What exactly is a Rule anyway? And who is Benedict, and what does the life of a monk have to do with mine, since I am not one and do not believe that I am called to be one.*

"It is going to be okay," I tell them. "You are not coming to listen to me anyway. People go on retreat to listen to God. We are going to make room for that to happen."

Is there anyone here who yearns for life and desires to see good days?

Whenever I read that question in the preface to Saint Benedict's Rule, it never fails to make my heart jump a little. I even raise my hand sometimes, or at least I do in my mind. I believe that I am not the only one who feels inclined to raise a hand in response.

3

I am in search of good days, but no more or less than you and the person standing next to you are. I am also in search of enough good days to make a life, maybe even a good life.

"We live our lives in search," wrote Frederick Buechner once. We search, he wrote, "for a self to be, for other selves to love, and for work to do." These are not new things that we moderns are searching for; they are as old as the hills.

The struggle to find others with whom we can share our lives, others who give our lives texture and color and meaning, has been going on forever. The task of finding work to do that is fulfilling and productive and sufficient for our needs has been constant. The need for rest and sustenance and time apart has been never-ending. Our hope and our yearning and our desire for God, and a life lived with God, have been everlasting, from age to age.

The world is not a simple place. It never really was. But it is clear that with the noise and the pace and the demands of life in the information age—if that is still the name for the age in which we are living—the struggle to balance all of those things becomes more and more difficult, and more and more necessary.

We are asked by the communities of which we are a part—our families, our neighborhoods, our churches, and all the rest—to do more, not less. In the places where we work, we are asked to be more productive, more efficient, to work longer and harder. We are seldom encouraged to rest and we are seldom asked to slow down.

4

We are bombarded by information and by noise, and we are conflicted by our priorities and our choices and our time constraints. We are given lots of power tools—faxes and computers and telephones and automobiles—and yet we still have only the one mind and the one heart and the one spirit. We have only a certain amount of strength and a finite number of hours in the day and these two hands.

How then to wrestle with all of these things, how then to wrestle our way into a life of good days that will yield up some sense of the life for which we yearn? How then to balance all of these competing voices and demands and tensions—some of them good, some of them not so good, and some of them simply omnipresent—with our longing to be with God?

In a world that keeps asking us to go higher and faster, how do we begin to go deeper, into the place where God lives and moves and has his being within us?

In order to begin to see your life as a whole, you must first take it apart. That is what we try to begin to do at the retreats.

The days of the retreats are shaped by the rhythm of daily prayers and set times for meals and silence and rest. In between, during the hours set aside for working, we do the work of writing down as clearly and simply as we can the way we actually spend our lives. And we begin to compare those notes with the way we want to live out our callings and be with our communities and offer our prayer.

The first thing that we do is to divide our lives into four pieces—prayer, rest, community, and work. Now I know how hard it is to do that arbitrarily.

Where do I put the people that I work with and where do I put my church stuff? Where does the family vacation go, and is a retreat a prayer thing or a rest thing? If I wash the dishes every night, is that work or is it community?

People in the retreat are drawing these little charts and asking where to put stuff, and I try to be as unhelpful as I can, as kindly as I can, of course. It helps not to be a scholar or a teacher at this point, because then I can more easily say that I do not know where those things go on your charts. What I do know is that you have to take all of them into account. What I am sure of is this: All of the bits and pieces of our lives, large and small, must be held up in the light of our longing to live for and with God.

After the charts, we begin to wrestle with another set of questions: Name the things that you do each day, each week, each month, each year that you consider to be prayer. How long does each of those things take and how faithful to them are you? How faithful are you in reality (as opposed to how faithful to them that you want to be or promised to be)?

The questions keep coming: What is your current experience of those things? Are they dry and lifeless to you or are they rich and deepening to you? Why do you do them and should you continue them? Are they habits of the heart for you still or are they simply habits?

Which of them would you keep and why? Which ones would you set aside or reshape in some way or another? Are there practices for prayer that you have heard of or read about or even tried a few times that you would like to add to your own life of prayer? What would it take in terms of time and resources to be able to make those changes or add those practices?

We sort through the same questions about our habits for rest and for community and for work. It is a simple sort of process, but not necessarily an easy one.

"The Lord waits for us daily to translate his teachings into action," wrote Saint Benedict in his Rule.

"How we spend our day is, of course," writes Annie Dillard, "how we spend our lives. What we do with this hour, and that one, is what we are doing. A schedule defends us from chaos and whim. It is a net for catching days."

"Your way of acting should be different from the world's way," Benedict wrote. "The love of Christ must come before all else." And something in my heart says yes. But very often my life, something, or a whole host of somethings, says something else altogether.

So here I stand, with one foot in the past, and one foot in the present, headed toward a future that is only going to get faster even as some of us get slower. I am perched somewhere between the old-fashioned and the newfangled. And I am not alone in that, either.

So I have taken up traveling in the company of a sixth-century monk named Benedict. He is remembered because of the rule that he wrote for the monks of Monte Cassino. "It is called a rule," Benedict wrote, "because it regulates the lives of those who obey it." It has come to be the most influential rule of all for the Christian monastic world.

Which begs the question, of course: What does it have to do with the lives of those of us who live in the twenty-first century who are not monks and are not even planning to be?

I have come to see this "little rule for beginners," as Benedict called it himself, as almost three different little books.

In the first place, it is a detailed guidebook for running a monastery. It proscribes the details of accepting newcomers, when and where people are to sleep, when the meals will be taken and under what circumstances. It describes the roles of certain persons of authority within the monastery and what their jobs are and how they are to relate to the others. It sets out the rules and practices for everything from receiving mail and visitors, to taking care of the sick and the used clothing, to the times and the disciplines for saying the prayers that are at the heart of monastic life.

This first "book," if you will, has been the starting point for various and sundry monastic orders throughout the world over hundreds of years. In our time, a visit to any Benedictine monastery in the world will reveal a striking parallel between the shape of contemporary monastic life and the life of those first monks under Benedict's care. It has, no doubt, been transposed here and there to account for the monastic life in a modern age, but it is still read through and discussed and wrestled with by those who are called to live the monastic life.

This second way of reading Benedict's Rule is to read it and study it as a spiritual guidebook, a book that speaks very plainly about the life of the spirit.

Benedict writes very directly about prayer and its fruits and its practice. He speaks clearly about obedience and humility and service and discipline. He talks of devotion and of self-giving, of confession and of compassion, of the longing for God and the realities of living.

The third "book" is Benedict's call to his monks to live out the gospel in everything that they do. That is the book that catches my attention. For even though I am not called to live the life of a monk, I am called to live a life that becomes the gospel. I too am called to pray without ceasing. I too long to be the sort of person who brings honor and glory to the kingdom by the way that I live my life.

And I am not alone in these desires, either.

I actually did think I was going to be a monk once.

In the late 1980s, I was accepted into and began to attend the Academy for Spiritual Formation. It is a two-year program that involved my going away to a retreat setting with a small community of sixty people, four times a year for a week at a time. Each day we prayed the liturgy of the hours, set specific times for silence and instruction and reflection, shared meals while listening in silence to holy reading, and met in small groups to process the day's teaching and experiences in particular and the inner life in general.

Though I did not know it at the time that I began the Academy, the daily rhythm of the program was based, in part, on retreat experiences within Benedictine monasteries. I was immediately aware, however, that something deep within me was responding to it. It was a case of the longing of my heart encountering a structure that nurtured and fulfilled that longing at the same time.

In the course of the two years, as various teachers and priests and other learned folks came to teach us about the history and practice of Christian contemplative prayer, one began to read and to fall under the influence of some of the great figures of the inner life. Saint Benedict's Rule eventually turned up, and when I read it, there was such a clear connection between Benedict's words and the longing of my heart that I was sure that the only way to respond was to become a monk. (At least, I was sure for a little while.)

Over time, I realized that I was not called to live in the monastery, but I learned that I could live the monastic life interiorly. I began to realize that there were deep truths in Benedict's Rule that were still as meaningful, and as applicable, for me as they were for those who *do* live in a monastery.

The more that I read the Rule—and one can read it over often, given its short length—the more I saw that the Rule of Saint Benedict held within it a way of learning to balance the areas of my life so that I might actually become a person of prayer. I began to see—in between the lines about how to elect an abbot and how many letters a monk was allowed to receive and what time monks were supposed to go to prayers in the summer—a way of seeing my life as a whole. I began to see that one might construct a way of living that no longer separated one's spiritual life from the rest of one's life.

The more that I studied and talked and asked questions about the Rule of Benedict, the more I found that there were other lay people in the world who had found such truths as well.

The first such person I met through the pages of a book was a Memphis lawyer named John McQuiston. He wrote a modified Benedictine Rule of his own in a book called *Always We Begin Again*. Then a friend gave me a copy of *Living with Contradiction*, a delightful set of meditations on the Rule by a Welsh Anglican named Esther de Waal. Later I wandered into a copy of Elizabeth Canham's *Heart Whispers: Benedictine Wisdom for Today*. These are not the only such friends that I have found, or the last (I hope), but they are among those who are the most gracious and graceful on their pages.

The notion of living by a rule of some sort is not an easy one for us twenty-first-century Westerners to accept. We are generally too independent, too strong-willed, too mobile to be very interested at all in the idea of something that controls and shapes the way that we live out the days of our lives. We see ourselves as captains of our own ships, masters of our own fates, and we are apt to grow fierce at the notion that we are being controlled or ruled by anyone or anything.

Such resistance makes us the perfect target to be held under the sway of a rule of some sort without our even knowing it.

Given the nature of our society and its habits and patterns for work and school and transportation and holidays, a fair amount of our lives is under the influence of a rule that is not of our own choosing, whether we are willing to admit it or not.

Our jobs, our schools, our churches, our relationships all dictate to us the daily and weekly shape of our lives. They proscribe when we get up in the morning, when we eat, when we arrive home, how long it takes us to make the trip, and which days of which weeks we have to do certain things.

They have a direct effect one way or another on the ways that we allocate all of our resources, including our time and our energy, for the largest part of our days.

Those closest to us have a certain kind of hold on us as well. Any part of the crowd of significant others in our lives is demanding of our time and energy. Their lives and ours, by virtue of our relationship, are structured and shaped by the call to be in the relationship in the first place and our desire to be attentive to it.

To fail to notice the reality of such things is to have our heads in the sand, to believe in an illusion about the amount of control that we have over our lives.

I am not saying that these relationships and commitments are all bad things, only that their hold on us is a reality and that any one of us who seeks to live a life of attention to God must take them into account.

And in so doing, we must acknowledge that they do not always take into account our needs for rest and for prayer. They do not always take into account our longing to be with God.

It is the Rule of Saint Benedict that does take these things into account. It gives us a glimpse of how to balance our lives between prayer and work and community and rest. Thomas More, a writer who lived in the monastic world, said, "In the midst of our lives we can live the spirit of this rule." More and more, I am coming to see that is true. And that it can change us.

I am still trying to learn to turn my longing for the presence of God at all times into something that more closely resembles being aware of the presence of God in all things. And to learn how to order my life in such a way that there is balance between my prayer and my rest and my work and my community. And to go from working without stopping to praying without ceasing.

And I am convinced that there are some secrets hidden in the writings of an old monk.

Prayer

We believe that the divine presence is everywhere and that in every place the eyes of the Lord are watching the good and the wicked. But beyond the least doubt we should believe this to be especially true when we pray.

Let us consider, then, how we ought to behave in the presence of God, and let us offer our prayer in such a way that our minds are in harmony with our voices.

We must know that God regards our purity of heart and tears of compunction, not our many words. Prayer should therefore be short and pure, unless perhaps it is prolonged under the inspiration of divine grace. In community, however, prayer should always be brief.

On hearing the signal for an hour of prayer, we immediately set aside what we have in hand and go with utmost speed, yet with gravity and without giving occasion for frivolity. Indeed, nothing is to be preferred to the Work of God.

Those who work so far away that they cannot return to the oratory at the proper time are to perform the Work of God where they are. So too, those who must travel are not to omit the prescribed hours but to observe them as best they can, not neglecting their measure of service.

After the Work of God, all should leave in complete silence and with reverence for God, so that a brother who may wish to pray alone will not be disturbed by the insensitivity of another. Moreover, if at other times someone wishes to pray privately, he may simply go in and pray, not in a loud voice, but with tears and heartfelt devotion.

Whenever we want to ask a favor of some powerful man, we do it humbly, and respectfully, for fear of presumption. How much more important, then, to lay our petitions before the Lord God of all things with the utmost humility and sincere devotion.

— From the Rule of Saint Benedict

O n a spring afternoon not too long ago, I was in the back country of Louisiana at a retreat center for the weekend, waiting for the others to arrive for a retreat I was to lead. I was sitting in a chair under an oak tree trying to rest after the day's traveling.

It was the first warm and dry day I had seen in a while and I was enjoying the breeze and the sound of the birds. Then the bells in the church across the way began to ring.

The retreat center was attached to a monastery, and I knew by the time of day that the bells were calling the monks to Vespers, evening prayers, and I watched the grounds carefully for what I knew was going to happen next.

From all over, the bakery and the bookstore and the retreat house and the seminary and the cemetery and the walking trails and the fields and the parking lot, monks began to appear. They were walking briskly and quietly to the place inside the cloister where they would form two lines and make their processional into the church. It was time for the singing and the saying of prayers. Whatever they were doing before the bell—cooking or cleaning or digging or sorting or packing or resting or reading or any of the other things that it takes to keep a community going—they set it down. It was time for them to pray.

The following Tuesday, I was back in my hometown again, watching another crowd of people scurrying around at the ringing of the bells. This time they were high school students, and some of them were hustling down the hallway to get to a class that I teach from time to time at the school where my own children go.

It is clear to me that monks and schoolchildren have at least two advantages that I do not have. Someone rings a bell and they know what it is time to stop doing and what it is time to do next. And they have someone waiting in the hall to make sure that they are headed off to do it.

I am not so lucky anymore. I have to ring my own bells.

Some years ago now, back before I went to the Academy or met Saint Benedict through his Rule, or began to lead retreats or write books, I had come to a place in my life where I wanted to learn to pray. It was really that simple.

I had come to wonder sometimes at the lack of depth in my prayer. I began to worry, too, at the sense of imbalance in my life and at the lack of centeredness as well. I began to wonder if those things had a connection to my prayer. I began to realize that the longing that I had, and have, for the presence of God could no longer be filled by a few stolen moments of extemporaneous prayer. I began to have a sneaking suspicion that prayer was a larger and deeper and richer and more astonishing thing than I had known before. I began to desire a way of life that was more like the lively and reasonable sacrifice that is called for by the words of the Eucharist.

Although my life had been spent largely in the church and around people of faith, I had had a growing sense that I could go no deeper in my journey without some manner of instruction and experience in some ways of prayer other than the ones I already knew. "We fool ourselves if we think that such a sacramental way of living is automatic," wrote Richard Foster once, in a book about prayer and discipline. "This kind of living communion does not just fall on our heads. We must desire it and seek it out. We must order our lives in particular ways."

The call to "pray without ceasing"—the clarion call offered up to all of us by Saint Paul—had begun to ring in my ears and in my heart until it was no longer possible to ignore it.

Over the years, I have come to know that I am not alone in this call to pray any more than I am alone in being called to live a life that becomes the gospel.

So I went off to the Academy. I assumed I would quickly learn a few new techniques and some shortcuts and tricks to prayer, and that would do it. What happened was very different.

The heart of the prayer life that is proscribed by the Rule of Benedict is known as the *Opus Dei*—the Work of God. As time has gone along, I sometimes think that phrase means it is the work that we are to do for God, and sometimes I suspect that it means it is the work that God does in us. Both things are true, perhaps. But neither is true for us if we do not say the prayer, if we do not pray the hours or say the offices, or whatever term we use.

The Work of God is called by other names—the daily office, the liturgy of the hours, the divine office, fixed-hour prayer, and more—names that are virtually interchangeable in most of the literature about such prayer. The prayer has been shaped and reshaped by various Catholic and Protestant traditions over the years. But its basic frame and its role in the life of the faithful has remained the same. Thousands of years before Christ, the people of God—the Hebrew people of the first covenant—made it their practice to rise up in the night or stop in their daily rounds to praise the name of Yahweh, to give thanks, to acknowledge

God's presence, to seek God's blessing, and to offer themselves to God for God's work here on earth, if only by the act of the liturgy itself. And they did so by using formal prayers and patterns whose words were written and learned and repeated. They sung or said the Psalms. They offered prayers that followed the religious calendar as well, taking care to ensure that the Story that had been given them was not lost. They read the Scriptures as part of their prayer.

The practice of such prayer was a central part of the life of the earliest Jewish Christians. As the Christian faith was formed and shaped, they brought to it some of the ancient habits and practices of prayer that had long been a part of their devotion to God. For many years, this practice of daily liturgical prayer was the glue that held their communities together, especially during the time of persecution in the early days of the Christian movement.

When the era of persecution was ended, and the Christians suddenly found their faith had been proclaimed the state religion of the Roman Empire, they perceived less need for strict adherence to the prayers to hold the community together. They needed less strength to withstand suffering, and so over time they became less faithful in the practice of the prayers. The first monastic communities that formed in the deserts to pray, the *abbas* and *ammas* of the desert, were formed not so much as a reaction to the paganism of the larger culture, but rather as a reaction to their perception of the laxity of the Christian communities.

The ancient ways of prayer had gone from being a practice of praise and devotion to be shared by the whole Christian community to being a practice of discipline for only a few. Those faithful few kept it alive over the centuries. But even so, the divine office is a way of prayer that has been largely lost to us moderns.

Many of us are not even aware that such prayer was actually the prayer of the earliest Christians. Even those of us who worship in liturgical communities are not often taught much about it or even encouraged to participate in what the Church has come to call the prayer "that the Christ himself prays through his Body to sanctify the day."

It has different shapes and patterns and forms now, of course.

"Seven times a day will I rise to praise your name," said the psalmist, and so the early Hebrew faithful and then the early Christians did just that. Monastic communities still do pray seven times a day.

But in some places, especially where lay people are involved, the practice calls for four offices—morning, noon, evening, and night. In others it is only two. In some communities, provision is made for the offices to be said only in community, and in others the structure and the words and the patterns have been shaped so that it can be said privately.

But this way of praying still bears the marks of those ancient traditions. It is still built around the hours of the day itself—morning and noon and evening and night. It still has the basic components of psalms of praise and collective prayers for the people of God and prayers of petition and intercession and confession. It still has Scripture at its core, and it still relies on those ancient texts to provide the words that speak to and for the groaning of our hearts.

What does this ancient way of prayer have to do with us—we who are too busy and too frazzled and too harried in the age in which we find ourselves, we who do not live in a monastery but rather live in the world? Why should this prayer matter to us?

"The Divine Hours," writes Phyllis Tickle, are prayers of praise offered as a sacrifice of thanksgiving and faith to God. "To offer them," she writes, " . . . is to assume the 'office' of attendant upon the Divine."

The saying of the divine office—whether it be chanted or read silently, said seven times a day or four times a day or two times a day, privately or in communion, or in any variation one discovers to be the most workable in their life—the Work of God offers us the chance to make our lives of prayer larger than our own lives. The divine office makes it possible for us to be included more deeply in the prayers of the whole body of Christ, from ages past to ages to come.

It seems to me that all too often we all too easily make our prayer about ourselves, and ourselves alone. It is tempting to become the center of our own universe, and to expect

God to drop by on our timetable and to address our concerns on demand. And we become slightly frustrated or worse when the Almighty seems unwilling to comply.

Praying the daily office connects us to the whole community of Christ for all time past and for all time to come. It anchors us in the ongoing history of the church itself, requiring us to maintain the cascade of the prayer of the faithful, the Work of God itself.

The prayer of the office reminds us, too, that there is more in this world that calls out for our prayerful attention than just the bits and pieces of our own lives. The cycles of prayer that come and go each day and week and month keep calling others to mind—those who are lost and those who are ill, those who are alone and those who are at war, those who are afraid and those who have no home.

Praying the office does another thing, too, a thing that is perhaps the most important of all.

To pray the office is to frame the day with praise and thanksgiving. It serves to make the worship of God the center of our life. It changes the focus of our prayers from the created to the Creator.

"The Lord inhabits the praises of his people," go the ancient words. And the people who do the praising as well, I believe.

However it has happened, most of us attempt lives of prayer in some other way.

Many of us do not even know much about the offices anyway. We are not always taught that this way of praying is part of our heritage as faithful people. The liturgies and forms and practices have long since been dropped from the ways that we are taught.

And the first time we come in contact with such, the whole business can seem awfully cumbersome. How do I find the books that I need and how will I learn how even to begin? Is this prayer book or that one the right one? How much time will it take to say them each day?

Our lives are already very busy from morning until night—too hectic, it seems, to stop two or three times each day and read the prayers from a book or to say them from memory.

We live in a world in which we are encouraged to multitask, and to read books on tape (which is something that actually cannot be done, if you think about it). We eat fast food, expect overnight delivery, and sign up for instant messaging. We get too little sleep, have too many commitments and too much on our plate most days and weeks.

So we look for books that can help us pray our way to powerful Christian living in ten minutes a day, and we wonder why we are often left feeling somehow devoid of God's presence in our lives.

"Can you not stay with me for one hour?" asks Jesus of the ones who said they loved him.

"Can you not move a little more quickly?" we seem to be saying in return.

If it is beginning to sound to you like I am trying to sell you something, it is only because I am. And if you have begun to feel that I am preaching to the choir, remember that I am in the choir myself and have been in it long enough to know that this is the best way to get us to sing.

For centuries, the prayer of the office was at the center of the life of those who would serve the God that we say we want to serve. The people of Yahweh, our mothers and fathers, and the people of the early church and the people of the church across the years since—the desert monastics, the ones who kept the church alive through the Dark Ages, the ones who wrestled it through the Reformation, regardless of which side they were on—kept such traditions of prayer alive. They preserved the prayer, they observed the prayer, and they have now handed those traditions of prayer to us in our time.

It may well be time for us to pick up the mantle, shoulder the burden, take up the song, or whatever metaphor you want to choose. It may be time for us to learn to pray the hours, to do the Work of God—with devotion, with art, with discipline, and with care.

It is reasonable to wonder at the efficacy of such prayer, especially when it is unfamiliar to us. And so much has been written and said about dead liturgy and dry, rote prayers that we are right to enter into such prayer with care and with discernment. And we are certainly wise to consider the time and effort that it will take to say such prayer.

But we also should remember what Benedict wrote: "Nothing is to be preferred to the Work of God."

I have a friend who has a son who is in high school. Every morning he goes upstairs to wake him. And in an hour or so, my friend leaves his work in his home office to take his son to school. Every afternoon, he goes to pick him up after school or after sports practice and drive him home.

I know the son and he is perfectly capable of setting an alarm to wake up by, and the school bus stop is only a block away, and he has friends on the team that drive and live in the neighborhood.

My friend says this: "Whatever else happens each day, I know that the two of us, just the two of us, will be together those three times. I do not want any of those days to go by without at least those moments together." This, too, is a form of prayer.

"To love God," writes Frederick Buechner, "is to do about the same thing that you would do for anyone else, and that is to see each other."

If you keep reading the Rule, you discover that there were among Benedict's flock those who wanted to skip saying their prayers because they were out in the fields when the bell rang, or were on a journey and so could not pray at the appointed times very easily, and all manner of other things. All the excuses seem very reasonable and sound very much like the reasons that we might give.

"Above all else," wrote Benedict, "we urge that if anyone finds this distribution of the psalms unsatisfactory, he should arrange whatever he judges better." When I read between the lines, this is what I hear.

If you choose to say the office three times or four times or two times, if you choose this prayer book over that one, if your community recommends this as opposed to that, then so be it.

In short, we may wrestle this way of prayer into whatever shape makes sense for us in our time, in our life circumstances, in our schedules, but we may not leave it for someone else to do. It is the Work of God.

One of the lessons of the Rule is that prayer is not meant to be an attachment to the life that you live; it is meant to be the center of the life that you live.

And another lesson is that such deep and transforming prayer takes time and discipline and structure—all of which can be found only if one is willing to take specific and ordered steps to organize some of one's time and energy, one's hours and days around answering the call to pray.

But, writes Benedict, "We wish to set down nothing harsh or burdensome." We who live in the world are to find our own way to participate in the prayer that sanctifies the day.

"I must make my office with great care," wrote Charles Foucauld. "It is my daily offering of fresh flowers to the Beloved Spouse." An offering given, not for something in return, but out of love.

To make such offerings—morning, noon, evening, and night, or by whatever pattern that one follows—is to live inside the frame of the day that the Lord has made, to live inside it *each* day. It is a chance to recognize and to be grateful for the fact that, as least as far as you are concerned, God has indeed acted, and the world is indeed a new and fresh creation in which you can live and love and work and rest.

To make such offerings is to recognize that there is work to be done this day, people to see and to serve, those to whom you have been given and who have been given to you. There is room to acknowledge your dependence on God's grace and mercy and kindness as your day unfolds and its attendant work and struggle and joy and hope. There is a place to reflect on the closing of the day, to pray for sustenance and peace as you break bread with those you love. There is a moment to confess your sins and to ask for forgiveness and to prepare yourself for the death that comes with closing your eyes to sleep, knowing that only by God's grace will there be a world in the morning when you wake, if you wake.

Each day can be lived unto itself, not lived for the yesterday that is gone or for the tomorrow that may not come but lived for this present moment in the presence of God.

There is a church not too far from my house, eight or ten blocks at the most. Most days, or at least the days when the wind is right and the buses are not going by, I can hear the bells ring for morning and noon and evening prayers.

It makes me think of Louisiana and it reminds me of the high school where my kids go and then I think of my life and the way that it is lived somewhere in between.

The prayer that I heard said, or sung actually, that morning in Louisiana was not new to me in a way. I had heard it before in other times and in other places. It is prayer that is as old as our faith itself, older even. And it is as new as the day in which it is offered.

"The bells break in upon our cares in order to remind us that all things pass away and that our preoccupations are not important," wrote Thomas Merton once. "The bells say: we have spoken for centuries from the towers of great Churches. We have spoken to the saints, your fathers, in their land. We called them, as we call you, to sanctity."

The bells are calling us all, and that echo we hear within is the sound of our longing to be with God.

Rest

Day by day remind yourself that you are going to die.

Do not show too great a concern for the fleeting and temporal things of this world.

One must not be excitable, anxious, extreme, obstinate, jealous, or oversuspicious. Such people are never at rest.

There are times when good words are to be left unsaid out of esteem for silence. Diligently cultivate silence at all times, but especially at night.

There should be specified periods for both labor and for prayerful reading.

All things are to be done with moderation on account of the fainthearted. Nothing is so inconsistent with the life of any Christian as overindulgence.

Show forethought and consideration in all things, and whether the task at hand concerns God or the world, be discerning and moderate.

Arrange everything so that the strong have something to yearn for and so that the weak have nothing to run from.

—The Rule of Saint Benedict

For the last few years, I have spent the afternoons between the middle of February and the middle of May on a softball field. I have been helping out the local high school coach while he coached my daughter and her schoolmates.

One afternoon, at the end of practice, I heard a woman trying to hurry her daughter along out of the dugout.

"Why are we hurrying?" the girl asked.

"Because your dance class starts in fifteen minutes, and then we have to be at the church for choir practice after that, and if we do not eat now, we are not going to have time later. After that, you still have your homework to do and you have to get ready for bed."

The girl lives in my neighborhood and I know what time she catches the school bus. And I have a daughter about the same age and I know what time she has to get up to get ready for school and how much time it takes her to wind down in the evening.

The way that I figure it is this: The girl starts at about five in the morning, goes to school from seven-fifteen until two-fifteen, plays softball until five or sometimes six, and then goes to dance and church three times a week. Which means that at best she is home to do her homework most evenings around nine and is maybe in bed by eleven.

I doubt that such a schedule is what was meant when it was suggested to us that we train a child in the way that she should grow up.

One's work—whether it be one's livelihood or one's ministry or one's household responsibilities or one's schooling or education—always seems to demand more of one's time, not less. And our communities—be they our family, neighbors, coworkers, or faith community—generally will take as much of our time as we are willing to give up. Sometimes they will pay us more or applaud us more, and sometimes not. But they will always take more if we let them.

Time and attention are the currencies of our age. And most everything in our society—every organization, every institution, everyone with an 800 number and a web site—is somewhere right now plotting to get as much of both as they can get.

I once went for a stretch of some years in which I made a living as a one-person consulting firm that tried to take care of the dozen or so clients it took to keep my head above water and also support the half-dozen or so freelancers I worked with who were swimming pretty fast themselves. I ghost-wrote a couple of books in my spare time and had a small publishing imprint as well.

I was on the board at the church, taught a Sunday school class, and led about four retreats a year for the congregation, and produced all the promotional material for upcoming events as well.

My church life and my community life and my work life were so full and rich and productive that I nearly died from it. And by my own hand.

Other than the fact that I was tired and worn and sick at heart and depleted and lost and afraid, everything was just fine. And, of course, I had no one to blame but myself—even though I tried to pin the blame on some other folks.

It is clear from Benedict's Rule that he knew the power of the scriptural reminder that it is in returning and rest that we shall be saved.

The Rule is built around silence, to begin with, with a fair amount of attention to observing silence and protecting it for the sake of others.

There are also times proscribed for reading from Scripture and other works, as well as specific guidelines for places and times for talk or prayer or rest. And even though as lay people we do not live in silence, we ignore Benedict's call to silence and stillness at the peril of our spiritual lives. If those who are called and chosen to pray as a vocation deem it necessary for there to be silence and stillness in order to do so, then how much more is that necessary for us?

Silence is where you find it. Or at least it can be.

Some of us have particular places where the silence and

stillness are most apparent to us. A walk in the woods, perhaps, or through a park near the place where we live.

Some would choose a great cathedral or a quiet little chapel. Still others, when you mention the word silence to them, fix their minds on a corner in their home or in their own backyard. Or a favorite spot on a hillside or near a stream that they love.

Some of us remember times of day or seasons of the year. Times when we noticed that the world was a quiet place and that it welcomed us into its stillness. And that we felt at home there somehow, in a way that we had not before.

"We are fearfully and wonderfully made," wrote the psalmist once. And one of the bits of us that causes me, at least, to wonder is the part of us that seems to be drawn to the vast silence that sits at the center of all things.

I think about that sometimes, and I believe that I will never be poet enough to describe it.

But I have seen it, or the evidence of it: this deep connection to the silence, the "great Solitude at the Center of All Things," as Merton once called it.

I know that it is buried within us because I have seen its effect on the faces of those who open their eyes after a few minutes of meditation and prayer. I have seen its effect on those who return to the classroom where other retreatants are gathered after an hour's silent reflection. I have seen it, or sensed it at least, in the spirit—refreshed, restored, renewed—of people who return from a silent retreat some-where.

Even those of us who claim to enjoy the silence the least, or whose lives are the most filled with hustle and bustle and noise, have within us a longing to be still and to be quiet. It is part and parcel of who we are and how we are made. And it is a part of us that calls out to be claimed and cherished, nurtured and fed.

No matter how one lives in our society—married or single, in a large family or a small one, in urban places or rural settings, working full-time or part-time or only from time to time— there is not much call upon us to be sure that we take time for silence and solitude, for rest and reflection.

Our consumer society urges us to go and do as often as we can. And sometimes it seems as though every step we take leads to another step or six or seven, and before we can make one or two in that direction we are going further and doing more and trying to be something else.

I wouldn't dream of not being around the people that I get to be around. I would not want to try and find other work either, largely because of the people that I am able to meet and to know. I have been alone before and I like this better.

And I am perfectly aware that I am as fond of some parts of the modern world as anyone else, maybe even more so. I like packages that come overnight, clean water that comes out of a tap, automatic tellers that give me my money back, and airplanes that transport me home sooner rather than later. I like my *New York Times* being beamed overnight to the local printer by satellite so that I can hold it in my hands in Nashville each morning, I like watching the World Series even though I am not in the ballpark, and I like having photos of my children so that I can remember when they were little.

And clearly, as a writer who is hoping that kind folks like you will be able to find and buy and take home and read my books, I am a huge fan of all the technology that makes that possible.

But sometimes I am a little afraid that the world is going so fast that it will pass me by. Other times I worry that I cannot get the world to go away even on the days that I want it to.

But if the way in which I live does not have some silence and solitude and stillness and rest, then there is only one person to blame in the end. There is only one person who can, in fact, get me to do less and not more, to stop moving and be still, to slow down instead of speed up. And I am that person.

In the retreats I lead, we make long lists of the things that we do each day and each week and each month and each year in the name of prayer or work or community. In a sense those are the things that make up our own "rule."

They are the things that make up our "regula," as Benedict might say. They are the things that shape our lives. We may not have ever used the word "rule" to describe them, but it is what they are.

"From Easter until the first of November, the winter arrangement for the number of psalms is followed. But because summer nights are shorter, the readings from the book are omitted." So writes Benedict in his rule.

From Labor Day until Memorial Day, we go to church at 11:15 at our church. But in the summer, my life changes because Episcopalians switch to summer hours and go to church at 10:00. "After their midday meal, they will devote themselves to reading," writes the Saint. But not during Lent. Then they read in the morning and work in the afternoon. When Lent comes to my house, I spend my afternoons at the softball field. It is what I promised to do, and it is part of the rule that governs my days and my year.

Some of the things that regulate our lives are things that we can choose or change. Some are not. What is important is that we look at them from time to time and recognize which things are which, and which things can or should or might be adjusted in ways that help us to balance our lives.

Whenever we begin to talk about rest at the retreat, we all begin to fidget a fair amount.

The first reason that we begin to fidget is because all (or at least, most of) the stuff that we are doing that takes up so much of our time is good stuff.

If my child wants to be a ballplayer and a dancer and a singer and a good student and learn how to cook, too, who am I to say that she should not be given every opportunity?

If my church wants me to teach a class and sit on the board and show up on Sunday and bring my kids to choir practice and attend the parish weekend away and the fall retreat and the laymen's conference and chaperone the youth mission trip, who am I to say that all of these things are not things that I am being called to do?

If the place where I work and the people that I work with and the folks that I serve want me to work later and start earlier and come in on weekends just to keep up because I am clearly so important to the goings-on, then who am I to resist?

And if all of that together means I am sleep-deprived for long stretches at a time, or that I never have a chance to go on retreat or even on vacation, or that I have no time to think or read or study or listen, then that is just the cost. It is only my life that is hanging in the balance, or the lack thereof.

We fidget because we know that in order to say yes to our need for silence and rest, we are going to have to say no to some other stuff. And none of us much want to say no, and not many of us have folks around us who are encouraging us to say no in order to say yes to the very most important stuff.

If we want to begin to make some clear steps in the direction of the silence and the solitude and the rest in which we shall be saved, we ourselves need to make those first steps.

There is a class at the local high school that is made up of people who want to grow up and practice their art for a living. They are future poets and designers and musicians and dancers. They think of themselves as artists, and the class is about learning how to think like one and about learning the ways that one becomes one and still has food on the table and a dollar in one's pocket. I go in and see them every three or four weeks and we talk about such things.

One of the things that we talk about is the notion that there is a direct relationship between the quality of what you put in your artistic head and what comes out in your art. If you read bad stuff, you will learn to write bad stuff. If you listen only to bad music, you will grow up to compose lousy music as well. If you do not take the time and make the effort to listen and to study and to reflect on and to engage yourself deeply in the things that move you deeply, then it will be difficult to begin to make anything that will move anyone else very deeply at all.

Elizabeth O'Connor once said that we make the journey inward so that we can make the journey outward. She was talking about our being drawn to a deeper sense of communion with God that will somehow equip us and strengthen us and shape us so that we might be more like the Christ that we are to be for those who are given to us.

The truth is that often we are so actively engaged in our outward journeys that we have little time left to make inner ones at all. A few moments in a worship service from time to time, an unexpected hour caught in the middle of the night when we cannot sleep, the occasional long drive in the car when no one is with us and the radio cannot pick up any stations.

The truth is that it is far easier to see the God Without when we are regularly spending time with the God Within.

It is also true that if there is no time set aside for the journey inward, then there will soon be not much energy left for the journey outward.

A few weeks ago, I went off to Sumatanga in rural Alabama to attend a reunion for folks who had been through the Academy for Spiritual Formation. The Academy is twenty years old this year and so the people who run it planned a series of reunion retreats for the alumni. They held four of them, and one was held at the place where I attended my Academy some ten years ago.

Generally speaking, I am not big on reunions, and I do not often attend them. The organizers of this one tricked me into attending by asking me to read from my work on the first night. As my father used to say about himself, I will go about anywhere to listen to myself talk, and so I left early on a Thursday morning and headed south in my car. It is the best way to get there from my house.

The drive was familiar to me and I was happy for the solitude that came with four hours or so spent on a two-lane highway through the rolling hills of southern Tennessee and northern Alabama. As one might expect, I found myself remembering all those times that I had made the trip before and all the people that I had known there and all the things that had happened to me there and since.

An Academy day is built around the saying of the daily office—morning, evening, and night. Everything else we do is secondary to that one thing. And those who had organized this reunion made sure to structure it the same way. By the time I had been to Vespers in the afternoon, and night prayers later in the evening, and observed the silence through the night and woke for morning prayer, I was home. I was at rest, and I was in silence and in solitude more so than I had been in a long time. Longer than I realized, really.

The year that preceded the reunion retreat had not been an easy one for me. Learning to work in and out of a new set of professional relationships, a long struggle with some work that was difficult to do, a period of depression and lethargy that made it impossible to meet some of my commitments—all these and some other things, too, had taken more out of me, far more, than I had realized. And I had convinced myself that I could not spare a moment for solitude or silence, with the result that I had not been on a retreat for longer than I am willing to admit.

"Cultivate silence," wrote Benedict. And it is not always easy to do. But it must be done.

It is in returning and rest that we shall be saved. But not if we do not ever stop and sit down and be silent. In the returning to Sumatanga, and in the rest that was granted to me there, I began to see things a bit more clearly, to hope a little more deeply, and to be drawn a little more powerfully back into the life of work and community and prayer that has been given me to live.

Community

See how the Lord in his love shows us the way of life.

Show equal love to everyone. Accommodate and adapt yourself to each one's character and intelligence.

Imitate the example of the Good Shepherd who left the ninety-nine and went in search of the one who had strayed.

All guests who present themselves are to be welcomed as Christ. Great care and concern are to be shown in receiving poor people and pilgrims, because in them more particularly is Christ received.

Christ is to be adored because he is indeed welcomed in them.

There must be no word or sign of the evil of grumbling, no manifestation of it for any reason at all.

You are not to act in anger or nurse a grudge.

Express your opinions with all humility, and not presume to defend your own views obstinately.

Never give a hollow greeting of peace or turn away when someone needs your love. Do not repay one bad turn with another. Do not injure anyone but bear injuries patiently. If people curse you, do not curse them back but bless them instead. Pray for your enemies out of love for Christ.

Do not speak ill of others. Guard your lips from harmful or deceptive speech.

Live by God's commandments every day; treasure chastity, harbor neither hatred or jealousy of anyone, and do nothing out of envy.

No one is to pursue what he judges better for himself, but instead, what he judges better for someone else.

Let us set out on this way, with the Gospel for our guide, that we may deserve to see him who has called us to his kingdom.

—The Rule of Saint Benedict

When I was fifteen or sixteen, I came across a book that my father was reading. I may well have come across it because he gave it to me; he was forever doing that once I reached a certain age.

The book was written by a priest named Father Louis Evely, and it was based on a series of retreats that he gave in Belgium, if memory serves. In it, he talked about being the man or becoming the man that would meet Christ someday. I was raised in the church and around the church and I expect that it crossed my mind before I read his book, but I remember having a clear sense that I wanted to meet Christ.

I was not always sure in those days, and sometimes still in these days, what that might mean for me, but I have always thought of that book as among the first serious steps that I ever took toward trying to meet the Christ. It did not always seem so from the outside, I am sure, and maybe even less so from the inside, but I spent a good deal of time and energy over the next ten or fifteen years trying to meet him, and trying to know how to recognize him just in case he turned up.

In my middle thirties, my father began to write a book that he never finished. We did not know at the time that he was not going to finish it, but that turned out to be the case. By then, he had retired from his career as a publisher, and he was writing and speaking on a full-time basis, and he was working on something new as he spoke at retreats and conferences around the country.

After his death, we came across some chapters that he had written, and some notes that he had made, and some tapes of talks that he had given. Somewhere in the notes and the other things left behind, there was a title. *I Want to Know Christ* was what he was going to call the book.

The title stuck in my head and always has in some way. Partly because it reminds me of my father, and the way that I remember thinking to myself that he knows Christ now for sure. And partly because it seemed to me then, and still does now, that I have seen the Christ a time or two in the years in between, and I would like to know him better too.

47

Around the time that I was getting ready to turn forty (or as ready as one can get), I fell under the influence of a friend and pastor whose name was Russell. He turned out to be such a good friend to me that I would have jumped under his influence had I not fallen there.

At a given point, he was meeting on a weekday morning with a small group of us from the church.

It was a men's group, all lay people except for Russell, and it may have been listed on the church calendar as a Bible study but in fact it turned out to be a discussion group that was focused on our trying to tell the stories of our journeys with some measure of honesty and clarity.

Though it was not nearly as long ago as some of the other chief events in my life, I cannot remember all of the details. But one morning we got to talking about what we were hoping to become, what we supposed that God wanted us to become, and what we thought was the object of trying to discover and know the Christ.

However it happened, this is what Russell said when it was time for him to speak: "I want to *be* Christ."

It terrified me, of course, because I was afraid that we were all going to be struck by lightning. To say that you want to meet Christ sometimes seems presumptuous enough. But to say that you want to *be* him seems pretty far out there. I have come to believe that he was voicing what may well have been the object of the exercise after all.

My father and I were very close. We went to church together and we worked together. We lived in the same town even after I had moved out of the house I grew up in. We took vacations together and we wrote together some. We used to call each other on the telephone and read sentences, ours or someone else's, that moved us.

I remember still the first time that I went to pick up the phone and call him and remembered that he was not there to answer. I remember missing him. And I also remember thinking to myself that I would have to learn to be my own father now, so to speak.

Until he passed away, much of the structure and tone and tenor of my life and the way that I lived it reflected his. And in a way, I was not really a separate person. It fell to me to shape my life from then on.

Whatever I was going to base my life on, it was up to me to discover and to begin to put it into practice.

Benedict speaks directly to the abbot of a monastery by first reminding him to remember what the title itself signifies and that the abbot is believed to hold the place of Christ in the monastery.

And though not many of us would be mistaken for *abbas* and *ammas*, the truth is that we are responsible for leading our own lives. We are to make the rule that shapes and regulates the life that we live.

Whether we are male or female, married or single, live with or without children, we have a leading role in leading our household. "Let us set out," writes Benedict, "with the Gospels for our guide. See how the Lord himself shows the way."

The word "abbot," of course, is built from the word *abba*, which means "father." The image is not a hard one for me to understand given my father's role in my life and the fact that I am a father myself. I want to say very carefully and clearly that I know that such understandings are not true for everyone. But *abbess* and *amma* are fine words to me.

We are to "imitate the loving example of the Good Shepherd," and remember that "anyone undertaking the charge of souls must be ready to account for them." We are to "remember what he is and remember what he is called, aware that more will be expected of those to whom more has been entrusted." To "know what a difficult and demanding burden he has undertaken: directing souls and serving a variety of temperaments, coaxing, reproving, and encouraging them as appropriate."

I want to say this just as carefully, to be sure, but in addition to our spouses and our children or whatever crowd of folks turns up when we start naming our significant others, there are people outside that immediate circle who count on us to try and say and be something helpful to them from time to time on their journey. As humbling as it is to us, there are people who look at us in the hopes that we know something about this thing or that thing they are facing in their lives. It can help to keep Benedict's words in our heads and in our hearts when we are with them.

Because we are to be Christ to them.

But *our* being Christ is not the only way that the Christ appears in the life of a community.

"All who present themselves are to be welcomed as Christ," writes Benedict.

"When did we see you?" asked the disciples.

Perhaps "every day" is the answer. At the door and in the neighborhood and at the corner. At the breakfast table and in the back seat and on the bus. In the break room and the grocery store. Naked and lonely and sick and imprisoned and thirsty and hungry covers a lot of ground, you know.

Benedict calls us to a constant awareness that those who enter our world are all to be treated as though they were the Christ. He calls us to a posture, a way of seeing and of welcoming and of serving that is rooted in the sense of adoration of the Christ that is present in us all.

He calls for particular honor and care to be given to the poor, the sick, the needy, the guest, and the pilgrims. And who among us, who among those we know, who among those we shall meet tomorrow is not some or all or each at some time or all of the time?

The Rule calls us to order our lives and to maintain a sensibility for others that keeps us aware of and reflects the presence of the Christ among us always. Whether they live down the hall from us or are yet a stranger to us does not matter. The Christ among us is always to be honored, in things both great and small.

That sensibility can be nurtured, must be nurtured.

It can come through studying the Gospels, of course, by learning to see and to hear the stories of Jesus among us in ever-deepening ways.

And it can be nurtured by following closely the calendar of the Church, the liturgical calendar as it is known. Participating in its seasonal rituals and ceremonies can open our hearts to the ways of the Christ.

The awareness of Christ's presence among us can also be fed by simple and seemingly ordinary things as well. Looking people in the eye when you talk to them and listening carefully to the things that they say. Watching them carefully as they go in and out of your life, looking for the bits and pieces of their behavior that remind you of what you have learned about Christ in your study of his story.

It requires some slowing down in a way, being more gentle and more open. It takes some patience and discernment, and willingness to believe that one is actually going to see him. A little childlike faith, perhaps.

But if we are not looking for the One who came among us, then for whom are we looking anyway?

Some years ago now, a friend of mine handed me a copy of a little book by a man named Paul Marechal. The title is

Dancing Madly Backwards. I am not sure exactly which one of those words in the title made my friend think of me. I do not dance. Or at least I do not dance unless it is absolutely necessary or my team wins the World Series.

One of the things described in the book had to do with a word—*namaste*—that comes from the Eastern religious traditions. At its most basic level, it refers to the custom of placing one's hands together, as though a small child at prayer would, and then bowing to another person upon greeting them or upon taking your leave. As you do so, you say, "Namaste." If you do not say it aloud, the gesture itself says it for you.

In doing so, you are saying to them, "The part of the living God that lives and breathes in me bows down in reverence before the part of the living God that lives and breathes in you."

"All humility should be shown in addressing a guest. Christ is to be adored in them because he is indeed welcomed in them," writes Benedict.

"The secret of the ages is this," wrote Saint Paul, "it is Christ in you." And in me, and in everyone we meet. As Benedict encourages us, our judgment is that everyone who comes to us is bearing the Christ.

Most often, we think of this secret as the key to our salvation, as a way of talking about our having come to accept and acknowledge our relationship with Christ. Rightly so.

But there is another thing at work here. If Christ is in us, and if Christ is present in the others that we meet, acknowledged or not, then there are no moments in which Christ is not present. And there are no moments in our lives in which a posture of humility is not called for, no moments when welcome should not be the first thing on our minds, no moments in which we cannot see the face of Jesus. There may just be moments when we do not recognize him.

Christ is the old person next door, the one who fell on her steps in the dark and needs a meal every evening for the next month and has no family to prepare it for her.

He can be found in the face of the sixteen-year-old who lives up the street, the one whose father is a crack dealer.

Christ is there in the tentative steps taken by that college student over there, the young girl who cannot find a friend.

He is there in the joy of the young couple down the street who are out every afternoon with their newborn in a stroller, just hoping that you will stop them and share in their joy.

One does not have to go far to find Jesus. What one has to do is adopt a posture that allows one to see him.

My father used to say that when we get to heaven and see Jesus, our first thought is not going to be that we have never seen him before. Instead, we will grin and say, "It's you, it's you. I have seen you everywhere."

All of which, of course, changes the nature of every communal contact, great or small, whether we are being the Christ or receiving the Christ, or somewhere in between, which is where we find ourselves much of the time. At least according to Saint Paul and Saint Benedict and my father.

For Benedict, the called-for change in our bearing toward others is only possible as one becomes increasingly humble. And humility is most certainly the key to living in between being the Christ and receiving the Christ.

Benedict devotes a great deal of time and space to what he refers to as the steps of humility. Of all of the words that he uses to describe the proper posture for a life that becomes the gospel, humility is the one word, the one trait that he comes back to again and again. And, all too often, humility is a rather small word in the life of modern society.

The fear of God; the surrendering of our will; obedience; the embrace of suffering; patience amid hardships; the confession of sins; contentment with what one is given; valuing others more than self; submission to the Rule of the community; speaking gently and with modesty; the constant manifestation of humility in one's bearing—these are the steps that lead to humility according to Benedict.

Precious few of the things on his list are things that our culture and its institutions encourage or even applaud. That even holds true for the institution known as the church in many cases.

Throughout the Rule are constant reminders of what to do when strangers and pilgrims show up at the gate. Regardless of who they are or how they got there or how long they intend to stay, they are to be welcomed. "Proper honor must be shown to all," wrote the Saint. One has the distinct sense that one is called to include into one's community anyone who shows up, at any time, for any reason, in any state whatsoever.

Some of them have come to stay. Some will come only for a brief moment of respite. Some are pilgrims who are passing through on what Henri Nouwen once called "their mysterious search for freedom." All are to be treated with the same honor and the same respect.

For better or for worse, I have come to see—"am coming to see" would be a more accurate way to say it, to be sure—that my community is made up of those to whom I have been given and who have been given to me. And I am more and more aware that my community grows and shifts as long as I am willing to keep my eyes open—and my heart, too.

Some of them, like my wife and my children, will be with me forever. Others are from down the street or around the block, and my time with them will be gathered up in bits and pieces. Others are friends from the place where I worship or the place where my children go to school or the fellow pilgrims that I encounter as I continue my own mysterious search.

The rule that I live by for my own spiritual practice—the rule for prayer and work and community and rest—must help to shape me to be the Christ and to welcome the Christ and whatever comes in between.

Work

Hour by hour keep careful watch on all that you do, aware that God's gaze is upon you, wherever you may be.

The Lord waits for us daily to translate into action, as we should, his holy teachings.

Every time you begin a good work you must pray to him most earnestly to bring it to perfection.

Serve one another in love, for such service increases reward and fosters love.

If there are artisans among us, they are to practice their craft with all humility.

Relieve the lot of the poor, clothe the naked, visit the sick, bury the dead, go to help the troubled, and console the sorrowing.

Refrain from too much eating and sleeping, and from laziness.

In his goodness he has already counted us as his children, and therefore we should never grieve him with our actions.

Remember that with his good gifts that are in us, we must obey him at all times.

—The Rule of Saint Benedict

I was moving my office home from an older building downtown.

The office furniture that I was taking home was a collection of old drawing boards and filing cabinets and other stuff. My father had helped me tear out some walls and build a loft above my living room, which was going to be my studio. I did not know it then, but I was right on the edge of going from being a freelance writer of corporate communications to being a writer of books. If I had realized it at the time, I would have been even more excited to be moving home than I already was.

I had packed everything into a big rental truck the night before, and had driven it to my house and left the things in it overnight. I got up early, well before anyone else, under the influence of a kind of Christmas-like moving anticipation, I suppose. I propped the door open and started lugging boxes and things in the door and through the living room and up the stairs.

Once as I came down the stairs and turned the corner to go back outside for another load, I saw my three-year-old son, who had just arisen, sitting on the floor by the window. He was quiet as I passed back and forth with two or three loads of stuff.

"What'cha doing?" he said finally, as I was headed out the door.

"I am working," I said.

"Wait a minute, I'll go get my hat."

"Okay, pal," I said, and went on out the door.

When I came back in, he was upstairs at my drawing board, in his blue pajamas with the feet in them, with a pen and paper in his hand, and a stocking cap on his head. He was ready to go to work.

In the Rule of Saint Benedict, there are some key roles described for positions within the community—the abbot, the artisan, and the cellarer. There are some others, but these three are the ones that have spoken to me the most over the years—probably because I have a hat to wear for each kind of work that they entail.

The abbot is the head of the community and makes most of the decisions and hands out most of the assignments and is treated with the most deference and has the most responsibility. I am not sure that it would actually be fun to be an abbot, but I do like the days when I get to feel as though I am the guy in charge. (Sometimes it even happens one or two days a month at my house.)

An artisan is one who has some special art or craft they practice that contributes to the community life. They can write or paint or sculpt or build or some such thing. They are specialists in something that brings in some money to keep the place going or that brings some honor or prestige to the place that raises its visibility and reputation. Given the amount of ego it takes to claim that one writes sentences that others would like to read, you can well imagine that I am very happy to think of myself as an artisan. Even on the days when I know good and well that the sentences that I am writing may have little art in them at all.

The cellarer is the one who is responsible for making sure that the trains run on time, you might say. If there is no food, no clean habits to wear, no dishes for the table, and so on, the cellarer is the one called upon. I am a little less happy when I have to put on my cellarer hat.

It will not surprise you if I say that I think being a writer is a fine thing to be. Except for when you actually have to write, of course. Then it is about as exciting as washing dishes. Which is the other thing I do a lot of at my house.

I also mow the lawn, take out the trash, edge the flower beds, deliver the neighborhood newsletters, take my kids back and forth to school and to practice, and do the grocery shopping.

Some days I lead morning prayers at the cathedral downtown, and some days I travel somewhere to lead a retreat or speak at a conference. Some days I write letters and answer phone calls as though I were an actual business person, and some days I teach the class at the local high school. I paint fences sometimes, too, and trim the hedges for my neighbor and help coach my daughter's softball team. I do laundry in between paragraphs on Tuesdays, and I take the car to get serviced when it needs it. In the morning I pick up the *New York Times*, and I make the coffee at night before I go to bed so that there will be coffee ready in the morning when we wake up.

I wear a lot of hats. Just like everyone else. Some days when I have on one of my work hats, it feels as if I am playing, and some days it is the other way around. Some days I feel like a poet and some days I feel like a housekeeper, and some days I cannot tell the difference.

I expect most of us feel that way sometimes. Life is made up of a lot of good stuff and a lot of bad stuff, too, and in between you have to clean your room.

Some days I feel like an abbot and some days I feel like an artisan and some days I feel like the cellarer.

We live in a society in which work can be used to define almost everything about a person. Sometimes if you ask people how their day is going, they almost always answer based on their work. If someone's work is not very lucrative, there is a tendency for them to be a little defensive about it. People who have no work out in the marketplace are sometimes under the impression they are less of a person somehow. People who are unhappy at work act as though they are really on the way to something else.

If you read the business magazines you get the impression that if you work only forty hours a week, you will never get ahead. If you read the next article, you discover that those who work seventy hours a week are called names like "workaholic."

What the Rule says to us, I think, is that there are some other things to consider when we consider our work and the way that we do it and what it means in our lives. Not the least of which is this: Work never comes first.

"If there are artisans in the monastery," he writes, "they are to practice their craft with all humility."

I love the days at my house when everything becomes subservient to my work as a writer. Days when I am working hard on a manuscript or an upcoming event, writing furiously, being my usual brilliant self.

It is important then that everyone else who lives at my house put their plans on the back burner, schedule everything around me, manage it all so that nothing interrupts the flow of the brilliant work that is going on in my little studio. I say that I love it when events happen this way. But this actually happens very rarely, if at all, save in my own head.

There are moments for all of us, I suspect, when our work life is allowed to become larger than our lives in our community. We all have had some stretches when we over-book our schedules, work too many hours, take too many trips. We all too often have gone to work too early and stayed too late. It wears us down and it wears down those who have been given to us and to whom we have been given.

There is no doubt that work in our society is both necessary and demanding. Productivity matters and good jobs are not always easy to find. A fair number of folks are certain, and properly so, that the work they have been given has been given to them by God. There is a sense of vocation for them as they do their work, and so the work matters.

But it is also true that there are only so many hours in the day, so many days in the week, and so many weeks in a month. And the hours that we take from our prayer and our rest and our community because our work is always more important, or seemingly so, than the work or the play or the attention of or to another are stolen from them somehow. Those are hours that have been taken because we have decided that the work that we do is more important than anything or anyone else. We may not say it out loud, but we do not always have to; the way we spend our time says it clearly enough.

Benedict has a suggestion for those times when our sense of the importance of our work is out of balance. He recommends that when one "becomes puffed up by his skillfulness in his craft, and feels he is conferring something on the monastery, he is to be removed from practicing his craft and not allowed to resume it unless, after manifesting his humility, he is so ordered by the abbot." For Benedict, when it comes to work, just as when it comes to prayer, humility is the thing that keeps us in balance. "Above all else, the artisan should be humble," says the Saint.

Which would be easier if we had an abbot to let us know when we are out of line. But most of us do not live with an abbot anymore than we live in a place that has bells to call us to prayer. Most of us have to be our own abbot, even if we are not our own boss.

There is another notion about rule that Benedict brings to us. For those of us who are abbots for others, at least some of the time—whether we are married or single, male or female, mothers or fathers; whether we are teachers or pastors or doctors or nurses or supervisors—"we should always remember what the title signifies." The abbot is believed to hold the place of Christ in the monastery. And by Jesus' own words and the example of his life, the role of the Christ among us is that of the servant.

"Hour by hour," Benedict advises us, "keep careful watch over all that you do, aware that God's gaze is upon you, wherever you may be." Whether we are artisans or abbots or cellarers or some combination of all three, we are to see ourselves as servants above all else.

The picture of Christ that is given us in the Gospels is clear. If we are going to be like him, then we are to stop by the well and offer water to those who are thirsty. We are to wash the feet of those to whom we have been given. We are to cook the breakfast on the shoreline for those who have been up all night. We are to stop in the crowd and try to figure out who has brushed up against us. We are to keep our hearts and arms open for the children when they are trying to get our attention.

If doing such things in the world requires that we humbly recognize our call to serve others in all humility, then it is a proper trade to make.

It is tempting sometimes, or at least it seems so to me, to think of my work here on earth in rather large and grandiose ways. It may be that writers are the only ones who suffer from such a thing, but I am not sure that is so.

I like to think of my work in terms of building the kingdom and spreading the gospel. It is not a bad thing for us to step back and try to see how the labor of our hands and hearts and minds fits within the grand scheme of things. In fact, it is a proper thing to do.

But it is also right that we recognize that a goodly portion of the things we do that can seem mundane and ordinary are the very places where we are likely to live out the gospel.

Our days and our lives are more often filled with little chances to show our love to others than they are filled with great and grand opportunities. It is in those little things that we are given to do and to say and to be that we must do the work of building the kingdom.

It helps me to think about all that we do, things both great and small, if you will, in the light of Benedict's instructions to the cellarer: "Regard all utensils and goods of the monastery as sacred vessels of the altar, aware that nothing is to be neglected," he writes.

Perhaps the artisan's tools are no more important than that of the kitchen monk.

"I am as much at prayer in the clatter and the noise of my kitchen," said Brother Lawrence, a monk whose letters have been passed down to us, "as I would be after an hour on my knees before the blessed sacrament."

There is a blessedness in the ordinary things of our lives, in the ordinary tasks and conversations of our lives. Or at least there can be.

In fact, there should be.

In another place Benedict writes that "all things are to be done with moderation." He is speaking of the need for manual labor when he says this, that they must live by the labor of their hands in order to really be monks. But what I really love is the phrase that comes after "with moderation." "On account of the fainthearted" is what he says. I love it because we are all the fainthearted, to one degree or another.

"I do the things that I hate, and I cannot do the things that I want to do," cried Saint Paul once. He too was fainthearted, was he not?

Perhaps the answer for all of us fainthearted ones is to do less and not more. To walk slower rather than faster. To be more present to this day than we are to tomorrow. To just stand there sometimes rather than just do something.

Perhaps we need to remember that the work we do is not actually the center of the universe. The work that we do—whatever it is, whatever hat we are wearing, however great or small it may seem to us or to anyone else at the time—is to be done in the service of the Center of the Universe.

Living

Are you hastening toward your heavenly home? Then with Christ's help, keep a little rule that is written for beginners.

After that, you can set out for loftier summits of the teaching and the virtues, and under God's protection you will reach them.

Do not aspire to be called holy before you really are, but first be holy that you may more truly be called so.

And never lose hope in God's mercy.

—The Rule of Saint Benedict

On a Sunday morning at one of the retreats, after prayers had been said, a young man said to me, "How do I live my life as a Benedictine?"

"You cannot get there from here," I told him. "If you want to live your life entirely by the Rule of Saint Benedict, then you will have to go and join them."

He looked disappointed. I think he was thinking about his wife and children and his coaching job. He knew that he already had a place and calling to live out.

"You can live by another rule though." His face brightened.

71

"Live by the rule of Saint Whatever-Your-Name-Is."

He laughed and so did I. He thought I was joking.

After all of these pages of words about the Rule of Saint Benedict, I need to break the same sort of news to you who have been kind enough and interested enough to get this far.

The news is this: The people who really live lives that are regulated by the Rule of Benedict are those who have been called to live a particular sort of life, and have taken the vows to do so. You may well be on the way to coming such a person, but if you are not, and you are going to remain in the world like most of us, then you can live a life that is influenced by the Rule of Benedict, but not under it.

If you do not have a uniform, so to speak, you cannot be on the team.

I read a lot of Thomas Merton, and have done so for some years now. In fact, my experience is that you have to read Merton a lot and for a lot of years before you understand him.

"You are invited," he writes, "to cast your awful solemnity to the winds and to join in the general dance."

I take that as a heartfelt invitation. And, in the same spirit, I issue one to you.

The invitation is to take hold of Benedict's words and wrestle with them until there are moments that begin to reveal to you

72

a way to order your life in ways that make it more possible for you to balance your prayer and your rest and your community and your work.

It is an invitation to search the Rule, looking for the principles and the notions and the truths and the ideas that you can transpose into the fabric of your own life.

It is an invitation to fashion a way of living—each day, each week, each month—that is ordered and focused by and on the things that really matter.

"Work out your own salvation with fear and with trembling," wrote Saint Paul.

I invite you to work out your own Rule of Life as well.

Some people are morning people. They like to get up early, before the sun, and have some time in the dark and the silence before the rest of the day begins and before the rest of the world is stirring.

There is ample time for prayer and for reflection, perhaps in a journal, perhaps simply in stillness. Letters can be written and books can be read. Work can be done, the kind of work that is best done when one's mind is fresh and clean and uncluttered.

I am one of those kind of people, morning people.

Other people do not like to rise up so early. Even if they have to in order to be at school or at work. They really do not even want to talk to anyone much before noon. They want to stay up late in the evening, and read for a long time after they get in the bed before they turn out the light. The people that I live with are those kind of people, night people.

And so I have a choice to make.

I can do what I like to do best, which is to get up two to three hours before everyone else. Or I can stay up late with them, which I also love to do, and then just sleep in and operate the way that they do.

Or I can take a nap every afternoon so that I can do both. It requires a little planning and it means that the others have to agree to respect that stretch of time. None of it was hard to work out, once I knew that I needed to work it out. And there is the trick: Knowing myself, knowing the people that I live with, and knowing the longing that I have within me for a measure of solitude each day.

The prayer part of me needs the early morning hours for prayer. Those are the hours when there is silence and stillness, hours when the world and its noise and its bustle have not yet begun.

The work part of me needs to begin before the house is up and going. It needs for me to be awake and settled in at the board where I work before the clutter of the day has crept in. It is when I do my best work, and for me not to know that and plan for that is to be something less than respectful of the work that I have been given to do.

The community part of me needs to be with my family and friends in the evening. If I go to bed early enough to get enough sleep to get up early the way I need to, then I miss about half the fun and two thirds of the conversation that takes place at my house. Which is no way to be involved with a set of people that you love.

The rest part of me, however, reminds me that burning the candle at both ends is a losing proposition over time. It is okay for me to get up early and stay up late, but only if I figure out a way to get enough rest so that I do not drop dead in the middle of a sentence that I am writing or one that I am hearing.

Some months ago now, four of my friends here in the neighborhood decided to form a little group that would meet to pray once each week. They had in mind to say the morning office together and then offer prayers and intercessions on behalf of the 30 or so square blocks worth of folks that they consider to be their community.

They found a book to use, and made a commitment to each other to not only say the prayers on one day together, but to say them the rest of the week on their own, as a kind of communal act. Then they picked a place and a time of day, and set about choosing which day of the week that they would meet. Monday did not work since one of the four had a standing commitment to another group about the same time. Tuesday did not work because one person had a staff meeting early on that day each week. Wednesdays were out because of another person's weekly meeting, the weekends were not good because there was a fair amount of traveling to be done. Thursday became the day of choice.

Then, of course, spouses had to be taken into account, and children too, and a boss. It took some doing but they pulled it off for a good long time. After a few months, one of the group moved away, and then a baby arrived, and the season for traveling together in just that way was done.

For a time, a part of the rule for each of those four people was shaped to include a singular act of devotion and prayer, offered up secretly in the neighborhood, at the cost of time and energy. It was adopted as part of their individual rule, and then it was let go of when the season had passed.

One of the four of them told me later that what they had hoped would happen had happened. The act of committing to pray the office with each other and of holding each other accountable for it on the other days when they were apart had shaped them. It had shaped them in such a way that they could no longer go a day without participating in the Work of God.

I realize that such little bits and pieces of structure hardly seem complicated or earth shaking. I am smart enough to know that I also know that most all of us have the kind of organizational skills that it takes to do such things.

But I also have observed something else about the way that we treat our spiritual lives. There is this tendency within us sometimes, maybe more often than we, or at least I, care to admit, to treat our spiritual lives as somehow separate from the rest of our lives. We would not dream of going about our professional lives or our familial lives or our church lives in the same sort of haphazard manner that we go about our prayer lives. We are very careful to block out times and places for nearly everything else but we are not as quick to do so when it comes to our own spiritual nourishment.

There is something about the life of prayer, or at least the notion of the life of prayer, that causes us to just sort of wing it. It somehow has a place in our minds that is so mysterious and so otherworldly that we do not treat it with the same sort of rigor that we do the rest of our lives.

I do not mean to suggest that we do not care about it deeply or that we are not taking it seriously, but I do think that we need to be reminded that if this is the most important thing in our lives, then it may well deserve some thoughtful consideration as to how we will live it out daily and weekly and monthly in the season of our lives that we are living.

Seasons change, of course, even in a monastery. The Rule has a whole series of things that change for the monks when the seasons change. The workload changes and so do the clothes. The hours for daily prayer are shifted around because of specific work that has to be done. The meals change and so do the times in which they are served.

All of which suggests to me that from time to time I need to be about the business of examining my life and the way that I am living it. If for no other reason than to be sure that my rule for prayer and rest and community and work still makes sense in the light of the new days in which I am living.

Sometimes letting go of a spiritual practice can be as important as adding a new one. Sometimes reshaping one to account for a new set of circumstances is needed. Sometimes there is a hole in our spiritual practice that must be filled, and we can tell it because we are beginning to run on empty.

No one knows those things unless they have a rule, formal or informal, and unless they stop to look at it from time to time and make note of what is to be found there.

Only by taking our life apart from time to time and examining it carefully, and then putting it back together thoughtfully and prayerfully, only then can we be have some measure of confidence that we are living the life that we were meant to lead.

"Only he who obeys a rhythm that is superior to his own," wrote Kazantzakis, "is free."

The superior rhythm is the one that was made by God and whispered into us at the time that we were whispered into being. It is a rhythm that is based on the light and darkness of the day itself. It is a rhythm that supports all of our lives— prayer, rest, community and work.

It is a rhythm that is reflected in the Rule of Saint Benedict.

We are called to live lives that are shaped and nurtured and wrestled with until they become a prayer that is prayed without ceasing.

To do that will require a rule of some sort, even if it is The Rule of Saint Whatever-Your-Name-Is.

A Note about Saint Benedict

Before Benedict was a saint, he was a monk.

Benedict left his home in Nursia and headed off to Rome to study sometime during the reign of Theodoric of the Ostrogoths (493–526). Rome was peaceful then, even though the previous century had seen the city sacked on two occasions by barbarians. In the midst of the relative peace of the times, paganism began to rise, and Benedict became disgusted by what he saw and made a choice to leave the city and renounce the world and live as a solitary in a cave in a place called Subiaco, some thirty miles east of Rome.

As time passed, he began to come to the attention of those who lived nearby and to acquire some reputation as a holy man. At some point a group of monks asked him to be their abbot, a position that he reportedly took on with some reluctance. Whatever his reluctance was about, it proved to be well-founded as the same group of monks tried to poison him later on. (Monastery life is filled with more intrigue than one would imagine, I suppose.) Benedict headed back to his cave.

Another group of monks came to join him not long afterward, and together they eventually established twelve monasteries of twelve monks each.

After a time, there were troubles with the local clergy and he took a few disciples and moved some eighty miles south of Rome to a mountaintop, where he founded the monastery at Monte Cassino. He lived there until his death around 547. By the time of his death, his fame as a holy person had spread to the degree that even kings came to visit and to seek his counsel.

The Rule that he wrote to regulate the lives of the monks under his care has become the center point for the monastic life in the years since.

Notes on books and other things

Your reading of this book will be enhanced by reading a copy of *The Rule of Saint Benedict* alongside it. There are several translations available; your favorite bookseller can find them for you.

My favorite one, or at least the one that I read from most often, is the Vintage Spiritual Classics edition, Timothy Fry, O.S.B., editor. It was published in 1998 by Random House of New York. It is also the one that I used as a starting point for the paraphrase of the Rule that you find in this book.

There are also two prayer books that I recommend to those who are exploring the practice of praying the daily office. One is *Saint Benedict's Prayer Book for Beginners*. It is published by Ampleforth Abbey Press and is distributed in this country by Gracewing Publishing.

The second is *The Divine Hours* by Phyllis Tickle. It is published by Doubleday. Both of them can generally be found, or at least ordered for you, at better bookstores.

There are some writers whose work I keep turning to over and over again as I try to look at my life in the light of the Rule of Saint Benedict. Some are more explicit than others about Benedict's Rule, but I have found that all of them, even those who do not discuss his work at all, somehow echo his thinking. I recommend them to you, as they are fine companions for your journey.

Thomas Merton, *Seeds of Contemplation*
Annie Dillard, *The Writing Life*
Henri Nouwen, *The Living Reminder*
Frederick Buechner, *Wishful Thinking*
Elizabeth O'Connor, *The Eighth Day of Creation*
Louis Evely, *That Man Is You*
Esther de Waal, *Living With Contradiction*
Elizabeth J. Canham, *Heart Whispers*
John McQuiston, *Always We Begin Again*

The Academy for Spiritual Formation is an interdenominational program of the Upper Room in Nashville, Tennessee. They can be reached by writing to Mr. Jerry Haas, The Upper Room, 1908 Grand Avenue, Nashville, Tennessee 37212. (Tell them that Robert said hello and that I am doing fine.)

Last, and never least, I need to say thank you again to the people at Paraclete: To Lillian Miao for the opportunity; to Lil

Copan for her thoughtful and graceful editing; and to Ron Minor for his patience and hard work.

My gratitude as well to Ms. Dupree of New York, Miss Jones of Merigold, and to Ms. Green of Sunnyside—without them, there would be no book at all.

Study questions to accompany this book are available at www.paracletepress.com.

The author welcomes letters from his readers and invites them to write to him at 1001 Halcyon Avenue, Nashville, Tennessee 37204.

ROBERT BENSON is a frequent retreat leader and conference speaker. An alumni of the Academy for Spiritual Formation (United Methodist Church), he is also a member of the Friends of Silence and of the Poor, an ecumenical order of lay people. His other books include *Living Prayer, Venite*, and *That We May Perfectly Love Thee*. He lives in Nashville.